Perforated

Poems

Chloe Yelena Miller

LILY POETRY REVIEW BOOKS

Copyright © 2026 by Chloe Yelena Miller
Published by Lily Poetry Review Books
223 Winter Street
Whitman, MA 02382

https://lilypoetryreview.blog/

ISBN: 978-1-957755-64-9

Cover photograph: "Trees at La Pietra," Chloe Yelena Miller

Automatic
Elizabeth Colton Bonner (1976 – 1989)

At recess in grammar school, Elizabeth and I would whisper, "Automatic." This was our code to meet under the large tree at the top of the hill at The Vail-Deane school in Mountainside, N.J. We always returned to that particular tree to sit and talk. These poems return to the places and people who are my automatic, including Elizabeth.

No Matter What
Dora (Adea) Minnefor (1908 – 2011)

Aunt Dora would sometimes say to me, "I'll love you always and forever, no matter what."

Perforated is dedicated to Hans Noel and Owen Miller Noel, my automatics always and forever.

Contents

1.

2.

1.

Pantheon

My child's night shadow
on the Pantheon lengthens
into the *passato remoto*,
                    the distant past.
The past without our many lights
along the street, blinking from cars
and *motorini* speeding over the bumps.
The past of relatives further south,
dead for so long, their bones
were transferred, maybe by hand,
with or without ceremony,
from their burial place into a well
in the middle of the walled cemetery.
The relatives who didn't—
or couldn't—cross the mountains from Sala Consilina
to Naples' port, then cross the ocean
in the rounded bottom of a ship
to what became the home
of those who did leave.
The relatives whose descendants we visit
in their town built into the side
of the mountain:
                    Walls straight,
                    roads steep.
Their dialect relies on the plural
second person, *voi.* As in, all of you.
                    Even us.

Italian Vocabulary: *Intimissimi*

In a Trastevere church,
I balance a thin candle above another's flame,
lower the bottom between the metal netting

    until it is trapped
    into balance below
    the stone Mary.

What will they do
with the candle stubs tonight?
These handwritten wishes?

Twenty years ago, in Italy,
you sounded out the store name *In-ti-mis-si-mi.*
Intimissimi, Intimissimi,
IntimissimiIntimissimiIntimissimi!

    Laughter as repetition
    drowned meaning: *So intimate!*

I took a selfie with a celebrity today.
Thought of you, your desire
to be seen, known, and how
we stopped talking over

    what, really?

I light candles,
repeat *Intimissimi* until
we are again together
in our platonic love.

Impossible.

My wish, this clatter
of coins in the collection box.

Stars

"It's like a penny," she said once, eyes closed.
"No it's not!" the children cried.
"It's like a fire," she said, "in the stove."
    —Ray Bradbury, *All Summer in a Day*

Night, the child chooses one star. Stares.
She is careful not to move, not even to scratch her forehead.

    This star will fall.

She blinks, she has to,
and the pinpricks of light
leave tails. False comets.
When the child's star falls,
there won't be much time.

A girl shrieks that she saw one.
The child knows she chose wrong.

    This star will fall.
    This wish will come true.

There's still time.

Ars Poetica *or Pesca Tabacchiera*

Young, I didn't *kiss & tell*, but I wanted to. Especially after the first time. I wanted to ask friends if they felt the same here, there.

I still don't describe those touches, people, the light and shadows. I write around the center.

It's that Italian flat peach the merchant offers in a paper bag. He recommends a particular cheese from the next stall, points with a nod while watching your eyes find it.

Is the poem the peach you are about to eat while sitting on a curb in the shade?

Or is it you, holding a peach pit wrapped in paper?

Pomegranate

You identify the red flowering tree,
reach for a fallen bulb, pull it open
to exhume the seeds. *See, Mamma?*

This tree with its twisted bark
reaches up and out from our rented terrace.
I water it, another woman's tree.
Or maybe I shouldn't,
because of the drought.
We'll be gone
before the fruit ripens.

The wind carries charred plant
fragments and ash to our Roman neighborhood
from the wildfires nearby. A charcoal-black leaf
with perfectly visible veins and jagged edges
lands and disintegrates into dust.

I wish you, child, all the plants
and clean air, no matter who waters them,
no matter what fruit they bear.

Valentine for Our Seven-Year-Old

Even after a year locked down, after winter
turned the bare trees and pale sky
into black-and-white photographs. Delight, even still.

I want to write: Heartbeat once as rapid
as the smallest mammal he was, wrapped in polka dots;
innocent bowl of his armpit; impossibility of those knees.

How there was silence and suddenly: A human.

How he reaches for our hands at every intersection.

The narrowing eye he practices at meals when I remind him about vegetables.
The laugh that follows.

How he is often underfoot, looking up, repeating, "Watch me!"

How he looks for us when he gets something right,
wrong, or neither. How we're always there
to catch his eye searching for us.

How he's made entire worlds from one piece of cardboard.
How he runs across the room to launch a rocket into orbit.

How he calls us *Mommy* and *Daddy*, but writes *Mom* and *Dad*.

How he says *potables* instead of *potatoes* in our invented language.

How he wears a mask outside our home and has given up so much. How he listens
when we discuss the hard things, like *coronavirus* and *risk*. How he asks questions
and we try to be safe.

How we belong to each other.

Italian Vocabulary: *Guardare*

My son draws layers of scalloped plates on Godzilla's back. *You can only see parts of the plates in the back and sometimes none of them.*

There are things we can't see or didn't, like the moment the man leapt or fell from the footbridge over the Tiber River. But we joined the crowd watching a firefighter being lowered in a harness onto the grassy ledge. From between the plants, the man's arm reached out. We could see his forearm and hand before they fell back down again. The firefighter moved slowly.

Look how courageous the firefighters are to help, I told our child, while moving him away from the crowd toward the next bridge. *We're lucky to be somewhere with so many helpers.* He agreed and looked away from the river where tents crowded in the shade.

We didn't stay to see the man lifted in a cot, but saw the picture in the newspaper online. *Attempted suicide.* This was twelve years and two days after another friend jumped further north in this country. And a few years after a friend plunged a knife into his own heart. He'd been staring into the mirror, thinking about his lost loves, the newspaper reported. The article described everything someone decided my friend did and thought.

My son knows there are more plates behind the drawn ones.

We fill in what we can't see to understand

and wonder what's right.

The Bed Lost Its Lives

My Italian was rusty or
just not great. Study abroad
middle-management,
I sent M. in maintenance
a list of broken things.

When screws fell out
of one bedframe, I reported it,
replacing *viti,* screws,
with *vite,* lives:
The bed lost its lives.

We had a laugh,
but here I am, twenty years later,
remembering the lifeless bed,
thinking about what can go wrong
without the right words.

In this body

   I don't sleep.
Tonight, muscles
lock as I try to turn.

You died in the bed
hospice placed
near the front window,
three of us reaching
into the silence
to hear your breath.

Some nights my child whispers,
I don't want to die.

I tell the 3 AM streetlamps,
I miss you.

New York City (1)

The best way to get mugged, the guidebooks would admonish me, *is to look up.*

I look up. Follow the lines of the geometric sky rigged between the skyscrapers. I am distracted by height, the bird reflected in the window.

The poet-teacher warned, *Don't study poetry in New York City and write about the subway and how no one makes eye contact. Write about something else.*

I take the subway. No one speaks or makes eye contact. I buy a shirt with the F-word. I am amused by New York City, how it lives up to my expectations.

Georgia O'Keefe painted the city night between the blocks of buildings. Because of perspective, I know what's beyond the frame. My heart calms with her edges.

Twenty-one years after 9/11, I circle the ceremony. I have no family to claim; I am not invited beyond the barricades.

The bells toll. We face the new tower, silent. Then reporters return to speaking into cameras, but no one is in the spotlight. *Maybe this is exactly right,* I think. *All of us here, together.*

English Vocabulary: *To Mourn*

When my great aunt lifted herself from her chair,
thudded onto her cousin's coffin, and wailed,
I knew one day I'd fail her in my grief.

Years later, at her funeral, my cries turned
to hacking coughs. A cousin said
I'd ruined the funeral. Maybe I did.

I apologized, sucked on the acidic lozenge
she'd held out. What if mourning is my engine?
The engine of condensed time, sound almost

muted, just a whir, behind the t-shirt and jeans.
My hands do what is expected—answer
emails, wash dishes—instead of reaching

down to thump on the dirt or dig.
The earth waits. The engine whirs, here
and not braided together. It revs at night,

loud enough to crack foundation
until the deep waters reach sea-level:
Equilibrium. My son puts his head underwater,

snaps his fingers, listens for the muffled sounds.
He lifts his head, *Can you hear the sea?*

New York City (2)

Today's is not Caravaggio's light directing the traffic: *Look here.*

I don't trust directions. His canvas, large, the dark, velvet. David emerges with Goliath and the cloth embodies the unseen. I look to the edges. I wish I could unglue the canvas to see what he folded beneath the wooden frame.

This anniversary, I watch a child chase a pigeon. My frame widens, the light flattens. I look up. I can imagine what is out of view, but I still want to see it.

Returning Home

Leaf shadows speckle the stucco. I unlock the door. You take my bag. You slice the round loaf, flour on your hands. I mix sea salt, olive oil in this bowl we found in another city. The one with a low river.

There is much to tell you. I ate grilled fish last night. Even after dark, trees lean towards the sun.

Etruscan Bronzes

Facebook memory:
  I love you! I miss you! XXXX
with your name
typed, of course, no pen
preserving your smallest movements.
But still you, calling from the archives.
It had been too long then,
but now?

You loved a surprise entrance
like those Etruscan bronzes.
Noses, then cheeks, emerging
from thermal baths
unearthed while visitors soaked.

You'd approve of such luxury
amidst work, would have posed
clean, a closeup in portrait-mode,
Tuscan background only
a brown and green blur.

Those bronze figures,
from their height of youth,
artist's hand concealed
by the smoothing of time,
gaze upon a far-off horizon
long buried.

After I Die, Remember All of Me

This glass jar? I love
its ample, rounded bottom.
I love its small, glass handles,
not big enough to hold onto and lift.

I fill the jar with anything
that needs a container:
Beans, grains, chocolate chips,
coconut flakes.

On one side, the surface
is marred with glue where I tried
to scrape off the label—
to soak, freeze, peel, wash,
but these stubborn ridges remain.

I fill the jar again.

English Vocabulary: *Lentils*

Don't mention the lentils. We were poor and ate them. A lot. We also ate potatoes. Never give me a potato, but I don't mind lentils now. I also hate turkey, but that's another story.

I'll eat lentils with carrots & onions over rice or in a soup. Don't forget the olive oil, which is expensive. Save it for the end.

Poverty is a secret. It is. My father was good and worked hard. My mother found food for us to eat. She was hard because she had to be. During meals, she kept her belt on her lap: Ready.

I'm telling you, but that's it. Only you.

Can you keep a secret?

Butterflies

1.

He opened the low drawer to reveal butterflies. Yes. Yes, that's what he did. He slid the drawer out, placed it below a bright lamp. *My butterflies.* Outstretched wings and plump bodies ordered by size. Rows of butterflies pinned through the wings. The spotlight on the bodies, pins glimmering. *A drawer of beauty*, he might have said, but didn't. He was my boyfriend's father. I smiled at him, or maybe the butterflies, wanting to please.

2.

Over twenty years ago, I stood in the Royal Museum of Fine Arts of Belgium, fingers laced behind my back. I leaned into the paintings, never touching anything. One painting more precise than this room. Brushstrokes absent, as if a world had just appeared. Was it a woman inside, an expansive field beyond the window? I could enter, holding my breath, peripheral vision be damned.

3.

Today bombs exploded in Brussels. And, likely, other places, too. Today someone decided to explode himself and others. The explosion dismantled glass and bone.

4.

My son interrupts this morning's news when he calls, "Mamma, come here! I'm awake!" There is no television crew, steady or moving images, in his dark room. Only this: His cheek against mine, his arms around my neck. I hold him, welcome his wakefulness. He pumps his legs. He's awake, moving. Alive.

Light as a Feather, Stiff as a Board

Girls in flannel pajama sets,
we chanted in the suburban dark:
Light as a feather, stiff as a board.

One girl on her back, arms crossed
over her chest. Eyes squeezed shut.
The rest circled around her on the floor,
our first two fingers under her edges.
Light as a feather, stiff as a board.
Did we really want her to rise?

Of all the girls, I had the longest
list of recent dead. Alone in bed
another night, I'd cross my arms,
close my eyes, repeat their full names
just to remember.

News Since Your Passing

Your father remarried
after the divorce,
your mother writes to me.

And I miscarried,
tried not to believe
that baby was you.

I knew you wanted to come back.

    Have you?

New York City (3)

I remember being in my 20s, showing a friend around New York City. *That's the Empire State Building*, I said, pointing at the Chrysler Building.

I love

                you
before. Still. The you
on the beach
under the sun
sharing a lounge chair
with me,
your then-love.

That you is gone,
washed out to sea.

I am here.

But that I is gone, too.

Ars Poetica *or* The Burn

after Emily Dickinson

The man, not yet on stage, leaned forward to fall, not to follow a script, or modernize a tale or become a hero. It was high tide, a few cars with closed windows on the bridge.

Something unseen burned. Wind carries sound, flame. Sometimes, no one notices.

He dropped. Writers will describe the motion with words, notes, a role for the broad-chested tenor. They add an untucked shirt to balloon on the bridge from the electric fans below. Velvet curtains close before the drop, unless the theater can afford a harness.

The audience dabs their eyes, leaves the church, later the opera house.

They have questions, but it isn't polite to discuss the fall or how he was found. When. There's a family. They take bridges, wear shirts.

The writers look into the stage lights. There, every color of the spectrum. *Write it!*

The lights burn, repeat on walls, faces, sky, paper.

2.

My nostalgia

for your childhood smells like gravy
spattering the gas stovetop. And by *gravy*,
I mean that Italian-American red sauce
with braciole and ribs, fat skimmed
into a glass jar stored under the sink.
And by *nostalgia*, I mean the stories
you tell with cousins over coffee,
coats piled high on the couch in the next room.
Kids listen, look at black-and-white photos,
search each face for resemblance.
And by *stories*, I mean what you want to remember.
And by *remember*, I mean what you try to forget.

Italian Vocabulary: *Vita*

Pandemic height, we traveled to the bathroom. Our child pointed towards the toilet paper, the scrubber. Selfies with two fingers up, tiled walls behind our *get closer!* smiles.

Back in Italy three years later, he doesn't want us to be tourists. *I just want to live here.*

The airport taxi drives past a repeated billboard with a coffin advertising funeral services, later the Wedding Cake and tourists holding umbrellas to hide from the sun. I remember my American aunt speaking an Italian dialect. I remember helping to care for her aging body.

I taste the smokiness in my coffee. My aunt measured the scoops of her Folgers from a giant tin in her cupboard. I hum the jingle in the country her mother left, never to return. The country where her mother last saw her own mother. The line of women leaving while staying.

Across the street from our rented apartment, the morning sun lifts the yellow ocher painted on the walls of the Eritrean embassy. Sunlight can shift weight, density. This morning, the raised stones carved with shadows extend over the street.

Our apartment's walls are decorated with Arabic script honoring Allah in circles, squares and ovals. The far and near of this diorama in which we unpacked our clothes, allergy medicine, blank notebooks.

We find life in this light, language, the moka pot I use to brew coffee.

My family sleeps. Light paints ribbons across the leaves on the balcony.

What will we say to each other today?
 Will we look both near and far?
 Will we remember?

New York City (4)

When I peek into the church, a man in a suit encourages me to enter. *Queen Elizabeth stood here! We put this wreath there. Want me to take your picture?*

I decline his offer, take a picture of the garbage cans locked because of the 9/11 anniversary.

I don't take a picture of the plane that seemed to fly right behind, almost into, the new tower. It only appeared to, because of perspective and distance, but still. I catch my breath. I don't make eye contact with the person next to me, though I feel him looking at me after the plane disappears from sight.

I am afraid of crying. This is not my day. I did not lose someone twenty-one years ago. I was in a dormitory in Italy, running a fire drill, announcing that the students would be dead, *dead!*, if they behaved like that during a real fire. *Isn't this a stone building*, one asked?

And then all this time somehow passed and I'm here to feel something. And also, not.

Yoga Asanas While Pregnant

In Crow, balanced on loose
upper arms, my weight wobbles.

I risk tipping out of Tree,
prefer steady Mountain.

Called to Warrior, my legs
might fail. Inversions confuse me.

We are upright beings.
One day I'll be strong enough

for Boat. Future muscle
will support my weight, my doubt.

Before you unfurl, this body
is your home, builds

what can and cannot be seen.

After school

      I find acorns in your pocket
and think about how much
I want you to see the tallest trees,
the widest trees, run
down a rocky beach at twilight,
watch the Northern Lights cover
the whole sky like in the planetarium,
touch the aged cold of a glacier,
find a firefly—but don't catch it.
But the nature of my youth
is retreating, like the Dead Sea
and her salt pillars left behind
to stand like guards over
        what?

I think about the time I dropped
an acorn in your father's car, before
he was your father. A month later,
we saw green sprouts reaching
towards the window. No water
or soil, but life still grew.

Disarm

I was your home: Your limbs nudged my bones to make room for yours.

Now in the dry world, you walk, even dance. I am no longer your walls, roof, and floor, protecting your growth. This is how it should be.

I cannot save your body with mine if / when the shooter arrives. I cannot return to being your home if / when danger rushes in, knocks everything over.

You go to school to learn everything, like how parts make a whole and how your song and screams begin in your lungs with breath. No one can learn to be bulletproof, so you shouldn't have to try in the closet.

You deserve challenges you can fail at before trying again. Like building a bowl out of clay with two hands. If the walls collapse, you roll the clay into a ball between your palms, use your thumbs to build them up again. The clay may or may not become a bowl, but you can keep trying.

I cannot save you if / when the active shooter finds your classroom door, your desk covered in pencils and tiny erasers.

I must release you into the world so you can grow. This is how it should be.

And how it shouldn't be ~~if /~~ when …

Letter to Another Mother

It was practice, Mommy, not a drill.

We stand in a line and walk one by one into the closet. The closet is big. And dark! We can't turn on the light. We have to stay in there if a bad person comes.

A bad person is someone who doesn't belong.

E. talked a lot. He never listens! It was funny. My teacher didn't like it!

Scared? No, I wasn't scared.

Why are you crying, Mommy?

> *—My child, age five*

My dear friend, you are a teacher and a mom. You know the risks of going to school. Promise me our children will be safe.

I do not want to be afraid of school.

Tell me that I can stick with my old tricks – a towel over a door so my child won't squash his fingers if the door slams in a spring breeze.

Everything

Industrialized air snows
on ancient cypress trees.

I can't trust heart valves
and breast tissue,

only what I can do
or make with my hands.

New York City (5)

We grow up around belts like trees around fences. We cinch, divide our bodies into tops and bottoms. The sideways, metal *C* both cupping and piercing flesh.

I thought of Donatello's David, *S*-curve and all, that day you were old enough to get out of the tub on your own. You weren't bronze or wearing a hat, but you stood triumphant among the plastic toys, leaning on the sink instead of a sword.

When you stood next to the sculpture in that once-prison of the Bargello, I saw how little you looked like the crafted metal.

How my memory of both art and life were wrong.

Water Guns

The bright yellow water gun
can't kill, and we aim
at each other this 100-degree day in Rome.
Don't enjoy getting shot, Mommy!
my nine-year-old pleads
as he tries to win the game
with rules he made up.

It is too hot to do much else.

Elsewhere a father
bought his son a real gun
with real bullets
that killed real people.

We know too much and too little.
We know what guns are for.
We know what to do.

And yet. And yet. And yet.

English Vocabulary: *Grudge*

My aunt credited her long life
to codfish oil, dispensed by her mother.
We were lined up against the wall, mouths open,
like for communion. She said they each received
one shot glass full. She showed me how
they held their noses to gulp.
She was the only sibling who lived
more than a century, but no matter,
codfish oil it was. Codfish oil and the fact
that she never married. *No man*
pissed me off every day, she said.
But I credit her grudges. She packed them
into each new house with the fabric swatches
from dresses, olive-oil-stained recipes,
black-and-white photos. She never forgot
the niece who barely greeted her,
or the friend with the rough words
in the bathroom, or the relative's
kiss with the tongue she witnessed
while his wife was in the other room.
She'd point at the neighbor's outdoor light
to remind us how it was shining
right at her living room chair.
And there were more. I'm not yet
half a century old, but there's a global,
deadly pandemic. I credit my grudges.
I announce to my friend, *I won't forget*
who put us in danger with their
mask-less parties and lack of distancing.
Her nearly teenage daughter
shook her head, *You'll need to get over that.*
The kind child is right. Maybe
I will live through this.
                    Please,
let us all live through this.

Containing

In boxes: Shells glued to felt, once framed. Labeled rocks.

In a nursing home: Can we ship nature? Where would the parts live, far from their shores? The collector, now in a nursing home. The home, disassembled and rearranged elsewhere.

Once, in the night, a nearby house slid down the mountain, waking the people inside.

A parent applies for a pre-emergency grant for the future earthquake that might crack the school.

The permanence of shifting land; the stockpiles of stored water, the seat belts and zoom lenses to see what we can't. The buoys' height sounding the tsunami alarm.

Wherever I go, I watch people's hands. The skin that thins, while containing. What they hold.

The joke is

I never follow the instructions.
Me, the mom! Baking with my son,
I don't bring the eggs or butter
to room temperature, I don't separate
the dry and wet ingredients.
He's learning with me, despite me.
He reads instructions, stumbles over fractions,
laughs when I jump ahead, skip steps.

He wants to try cracking the egg.
Tightens his grip and it explodes
across the kitchen narrow enough
that all the walls are speckled with yolk.

We laugh and his laugh reminds me
of when he was even smaller,
refusing to sleep. When he'd play
peekaboo with chubby hands,
fingers wide apart so he could still see,
standing up in a fleece onesie.
I miss this child already.
His laugh might be the same,
years from now, shared with a beloved.

Baking together, we laugh
the kind of laugh that feels like
no one is left not laughing,
near or far from this kitchen.

Goofy's Sky School roller coaster

stops

        high

above where we started.

I mean, a roller coaster called

        Goofy's Sky School

    sounds less scary

than the others I'd said *no* to,

even though I knew I was disappointing my child.

The last ride of our day, I agree to try.

I sit next to him to comfort

    myself

    more than him

    and to disappoint less.

The turns, jerks, and eventual

stop in the sky,

      that is, Goofy's Sky,

         for *mechanical reasons*

    make me, the mom, cry.

My child keeps his hand on mine

when I should have mine over his.

He sits up straight, face turned towards me.

Sometimes people scream for joy, Mommy.

When he was a baby,
I thought I'd never be able to tell what his cries meant

     hunger   exhaustion

I surprised myself (and maybe him)
being right sometimes.

But here? These are strangers.
The park's hum of screams
so loud from up here.

But the Woman?

In a doctored image, an overgrown baby
tries to crawl from the mother's body

like a chick hatching from an egg.
But the woman? She's faceless

in this image held high in protest,
not given a voice. Her mind, her choices—

absent. The diary she wrote in, listing
places to visit one day, the ones

with rivers and history—missing.
Let her speak. Let her choose for herself.

She sewed

       two raincoat sleeves or
a zipper into a seam.
Each section produced
on a separate line.

I think of myself like that:
Pant legs divided from
my shirt hem
by the leather belt.
Two connected halves.

Seated, she watched
the other women
over the sewing machine.
Did they also want
to design patterns?
Did they imagine
drawing a skirt's long line,
standing or dancing?

Later, she worked
behind a desk all day,
cared for other women's
children in the evening,
and on Sundays
she danced in dresses
other women designed.

The day I knew

we were all dying
was the day she died.

She's the only one I write to,
the one who wore flowery dresses
when she wasn't at the Mayo Clinic.

Snow when she was buried
on that hill overlooking a curving street.
Five years later, old enough to drive,
I'd loop past her on my way to the movies
or anywhere, really, if I could.

Snow when she was buried, or
am I remembering wrong?
It may have been sunny or rainy
or any of the other weathers
that have persisted, impossibly,
despite her absence.

English Vocabulary: *Hate*

My son reminds me,
  Don't say "hate," Mommy.

But I do.

That red-chili-flake burn in your stomach
and sweat on your hairline
eats straight through all the love
I'm supposed to have.

New York City (6)

You are each layer, by which I mean age, at once. A palimpsest of sorts. You reach for my hand no matter what year it is or where we are, even if we prefer this street where we always walked. We see each other, while looking towards the trees reaching up in the woods.

We have this:

        made,

            saved &

                  remembered.

Italian Vocabulary: *Luna sul Colosseo*

Easier to imagine the giraffes, elephants, and lions transported on boats to Rome than the enslaved people used to build the Colosseum, construct the scenes for spectators, fight, feed the caged chickens killed for snacks.

We tour the Colosseum's underground beneath the moon, see the water used to move the larger scenes, the reconstructed elevator, even higher walls once covered in marble and frescoes.

There's no memorial or stone block dedicated to the builders, workers, or fighters. There's the Door of the Dead used by those carrying them.

A car race on the road above; cars screeching to make the hairpin turn. Sounds like the earthquake that knocked down some of the walls years ago.

The living city circles the oval of arches, a monument to the ancient past, reaches into the future past Covid, the lockdowns, the deaths. Our taxi passes a repeating ad for a funeral home with a colossal coffin.

Raised Architecture of Gold Leaf

Time-gone smoke darkened
any possible reflection. Museum light
and shadows shift the narrative.

Gold demands candlelight.
On second thought, maybe
candlelight demands the gold?

Unworldly background
in this world—time travel.
Trim on Mary's cloak, gold

hammered like the landscape.
Look longer and figures fade.
The repeating patterns

the remains of artists
who thinned, applied, hammered
this gold, (un)expected light.

When You Transformed My Poems into Music

You know how when you sleep too late
& you wake up to
light
brightening every crevice, bedsheet fold,
& you,
even with the blinds still down?

That is what it was like to listen

as your voice,

your notes,

filled the space between
the white walls. Between

my ribs,
the strings of light
                            vibrated

into that space between my ribs.

Happy New Year

I know better
      now
than to expect the perfection
of a new year.

I eat the lentils, the sausage,
and lean into tradition—and flavor—
rather than sorcery.

Zelenskyy spoke in his war-torn country,
      We haven't lost anything. It was taken from us.

Every day of every year, we make choices.

This morning I'll write,
water this African violet—
like the one my grandmother had
on her window sill—
and look for buds.

Palimpsest

If I were commissioned to design a church,
    I'd design it for you, child.

I'd set the dome on high ground.
    Nearby, impossibly tall marble door
    disguised by filigree carving:
    Ever rotating exhibit of light and dark.

Surface all texture and shadows. Stories
    wouldn't matter, just the shapes.
    Or are shapes only disguised stories?

Windows would offer the sky, inside or out.

There's no exact word to describe seeing through
    architecture to the other side.
    Perforated
        isn't quite right.

You and I watch the day's light shapeshift.
    What is revealed and when.
    There a bird's underbelly, here a corner
    before it becomes something smoother.

Silence and all the sounds of laughter and wails.
    This is, after all, a monument to humans
    crafted by artists and mathematicians.

Inside, all the books and grain, water and creatures.

We walk the Florentine street, holding hands.
    Mine? Do you have pencil and paper?

Coda

My littlest love,

Here, eat the hard-boiled egg. Don't forget the banana bread a neighbor dropped off with a note that read, "Grateful to be your neighbor."

Grateful. I'm grateful for our community, this food. I'm grateful the lockdown at your school on Friday was only "out of an abundance of caution," as the principal emailed. The gunshots were outside of another school, not inside yours. You were watching a play in the gym. I'm grateful the gym doesn't have windows. That you don't have a phone to read the news in real time. That I couldn't call you, crying with fear, like I wanted to. Like I did to your father and my own mother.

I cannot live like this, grateful for things that shouldn't need to be named. I keep living like this, grateful for another day the shooting didn't happen at your school. Grateful that we woke up, whole, yet again, and together.

Here, eat this hard-boiled egg and homemade bread. We have this. We have this day while others don't.

Others in schools, clubs, movie theaters, churches, temples. Others here in America.

Eat up. We have another day to live. And fight. The living is part of the fight. But we owe each other more. We owe you more.

Eat this egg, shelled for you this morning by my hands, still cold from the bowl of ice water meant to separate the egg from its shell.

Let us be together in this abundance of love.

Love, Mamma

Notes

Italian Vocabulary: *Intimissimi* and Etruscan Bronzes
These two poems are written for my friend Edward Wyckoff Williams (1978
– 2022). Trastevere is a neighborhood in Rome, Italy. *Initimissi* means "very
intimate" and is the name of an Italian lingerie store. The Etruscan Bronzes
from the second poem were 2,300 year-old bronzes found in 2022 in a thermal
spring in San Casciano dei Bagni, Tuscany.

Ars Poetica *or* Pesca Tabacchiera
The "Pesca Tabacchiera" is a flat peach, sometimes called a "donut peach."
The direct translation from Italian is "snuffbox peach."

Pomegranate
My family spent summer 2022 in Rome, Italy, for work. We stayed in an
apartment with a garden terrace. Meanwhile, there were periodically large
fires on the edges of the city. These fires might have been caused by arson or
drought.

Italian Vocabulary: *Guardare*
"Guardare" means "to watch" in English.

The Bed Lost Its Lives
I worked for NYU in Florence, Italy from 2000 – 2003. As the Residence Hall
Manager, I was responsible for writing many maintenance reports. Technical
Assistant and friend Mario Carcasci was a hero for untangling my Italian.

English Vocabulary: *Lentils*
This poem is from a recorded interview with my Great Aunt Dora. Melvin
Coston kindly helped me to interview and record her in 2004. Later she said
that I could share these facts in poems if I thought "anyone wanted to know."

Butterflies
There's a reference to the 2016 bombings in Brussels, Belgium.

I love
This poem is after Kay Ryan's poem *After Zeno*.

Italian Vocabulary: *Vita*
The Monument of Victor Emanuel II, also called the Altare della Patria (Alter of the Fatherland), is sometimes referred to as the Wedding Cake because of its design.

Letter to Another Mother
This poem comes from a poetry letter exchange in 2018 with poet, mom and friend Sara R. Burnett, author of *Seed Celestial* (winner of the Autumn House Poetry Prize, 2022).

Everything
The cypress is frequently paired with other symbols to express "many" or "everything."

Containing
This poem refers to a Portland, OR, house that slid about 100 yards down a hillside in 2008 due to a landslide.

She sewed
This poem is about Great Aunt Dora from stories she told about living and working in Newark, NJ, 1930.

Italian Vocabulary: *Luna sul Colosseo*
This was the name of the nighttime tour we took of the lower levels of the Colosseum in Rome, Italy, in 2022. The direct translation is "moon over the Colosseum."

Raised Architecture of Gold Leaf
This poem references gold leaf used in Italian Renaissance paintings in the 13th and 14th centuries. Thank you to Elizabeth Namack of My Italian Treasures for organizing a gilding workshop at Oro & Colore in Florence, Italy.

When You Transformed My Poems into Music
Composer Lauren Spavelko set some poems from my first collection, *Viable* (Lily Poetry Review Books, 2021) to music. I wrote this poem after hearing selections from this composition, *Baby Book*, performed by soprano Rachel Sitomer and pianist Ashlee Mack in Annapolis, MD, in June, 2022.

Acknowledgements

Thank you to these publications that previously published the following poems.

"Pantheon"
"Italian Vocabulary: *Intimissimi*"
   Earlier versions of these two poems were published by *Gargoyle* (February 2023)

"Ars Poetica *or* Pesca Tabacchiera"
   An earlier version was published by *Poet Lore* (Winter 2024)

"Italian Vocabulary: *Guardare*"
"Italian Vocabulary: *Luna sul Colosseo*"
   Earlier versions of these two poems were published by *Open Doors Review* (December 2024)

"The Bed Lost Its Lives"
"After I Die, Remember All of Me"
"But the Woman?"
   Earlier versions of these three poems were published by *Lily Poetry Review* (April 2023)

"New York City (1 – 6)"
   An earlier and essay version of New York City was published by Grace & Gravity's *Grace in Love*, vol. X (May 2023)

"English Vocabulary: *To Mourn*"
   An earlier version was published by *Calyx* (Spring 2024). There is also an audio recording of my reading this poem available on their website

"Returning Home"
   An earlier version was published by *Beltway Poetry Quarterly* (October 2013)

"English Vocabulary: *Lentils*"

"Palimpsest"

Earlier versions of these two poems were published by *VIA: Voices in Italian Americana* (Winter 2022)

"Italian Vocabulary: *Vita*"

An earlier version (previously titled 'Living') was published by *Ovunque Siamo* (August 2022)

"After school"

This poem will be published in *Washington Writers' Publishing House Writes* (February 2026)

"Disarm"

An earlier version was published by *Mom Egg Review* (April 2023)

"Water Guns"

An earlier version was published online by *Washington Writers' Publishing House Writes* (March 2023)

"The joke is"

An earlier version (previously titled 'Baking with my child') was published by *Mom Egg Review* in their "Mother Folk" Folio (December 2022)

"She sewed"

An earlier version was published by *Bourgeon* (later re-named *Mid-Atlantic Review)* (July 2022)

"Raised Architecture of Gold Leaf"

An earlier version was published by *Bourgeon* (later re-named *Mid-Atlantic Review*) (January 2023)

"When You Transformed My Poems into Music"
    An earlier version was shared on composer Lauren Spavelko's website: https://www.laurenspavelko.com

"Happy New Year"
    This poem was published by *Beltway Poetry*'s War and Peace issue (August 2025)

A word on the Italian and English definition poems:
    These poems are a part of a growing collection that span from my chapbook, *Unrest* (Finishing Line Press 2013), my first full length manuscript, *Viable* (Lily Poetry Review Books, 2021), this collection and, likely, future ones, too.

Thank You

Thank you to Eileen Cleary for your own poems and all that you do for the Lily Poetry family. Thank you for your trust in me and my work in this second poetry collection with Lily.

Martha McCollough, your covers are always remarkable.

Thank you to Maggie Smith for your support editing these poems.

Thank you to the DC Commission on the Arts & Humanities for Individual Artist Fellowships (2020, 2022 and 2024), which have helped me to make more space for writing. Thank you to my mother, artist Melabee M. Miller, for making DYI artistic residencies with me. I look forward to many more!

Thank you to Shradha Shah and Emily Simmons for reading earlier drafts of some of these poems and sharing your own during our virtual workshops. And to Amy Bucklin for your grammar and punctuation wizardry throughout the years and on some of these poems. Thank you to Sara R. Burnett for your support and willingness to share poems at any time. Stella Fiore, your leadership of Cut & Paste AIRM through the pandemic and beyond, as well as your friendship, has strengthened my resolve to continue writing.

Thank you to my friends, Alethea, Amy and Hannah, who always listen and help me to sort through ideas which often find themselves in poems. Ishita, I so appreciate you and your family's friendship. You've helped to make D.C. a home, even throughout the pandemic lockdown. This comfort helped me to have the space to write.

To my friend and Brown Bag Lit partner, Shasta Grant: I am so happy that we have each other as business partners, literary colleagues and, best of all, friends. Your laughter, listening ear and encouragement mean the world to me. And your "Shasta magic" is legendary!

To my parents, Melabee and Larry, thank you for always encouraging me to write and reading drafts of my work.

Thank you to my husband, Hans Noel, whose research and classes have brought our family back to Italy over the summers. Our time there is nourishing. I can't imagine this life without us by each other's sides.

Dearest Owen, I wish you the best always. I admire your dedication to your own arts. I'll love you always and forever, no matter what. May you always be surrounded by love, nature, poetry and all of the cheese!

Author Biography

Photo by Hans Noel

Chloe Yelena Miller is a writer and teacher living in Washington, D.C., with her partner and their child. *Perforated* is her second full-length poetry collection. She's also the author of the poetry collection *Viable* (Lily Poetry Review Books 2021) and the poetry chapbook *Unrest* (Finishing Line Press 2013). She and Shasta Grant co-founded and co-direct Brown Bag Lit, an online writing community. She also teaches writing and literature through University of Maryland's Global Campus, Politics and Prose bookstore, and New Directions in Writing, as well as privately. Miller has a BA in Italian language and literature from Smith College (1998) and an MFA in poetry from Sarah Lawrence College (2003). http://www.chloeyelenamiller.com